Reteach:
Phonics Skills

Level 1

Teacher's Annotated Edition

A Division of The McGraw·Hill Companies

Columbus, Ohio

www.sra4kids.com

SRA/McGraw-Hill

A Division of The **McGraw·Hill** *Companies*

Send all inquiries to:
SRA/McGraw-Hill
8787 Orion Place
Columbus, OH 43240-4027

Printed in the United States of America.

ISBN 0-07-572026-4

3 4 5 6 7 8 9 POH 07 06 05 04 03

Table of Contents

▶ Writing Letters

PHONICS SKILLS

Directions: Trace the first two letters and write three more letters on the lines.

A A A A A A

a a a a a a

B B B B B B

b b b b b b

▶ Writing Letters

Directions: Trace the first two letters and write three more letters on the lines.

PHONICS SKILLS

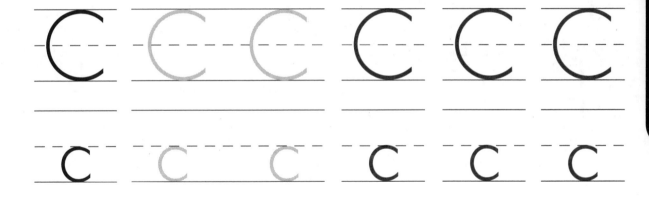

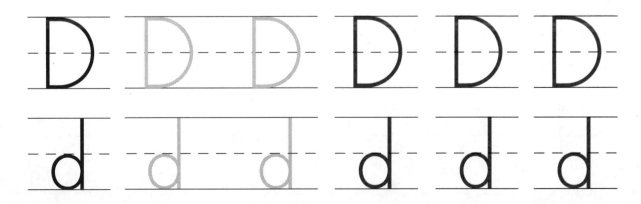

UNIT 1   Let's Read! • **Lesson 3** *Las hormiguitas*

▶Writing Letters

Directions: Trace the first two letters and write three more letters on the lines.

PHONICS SKILLS

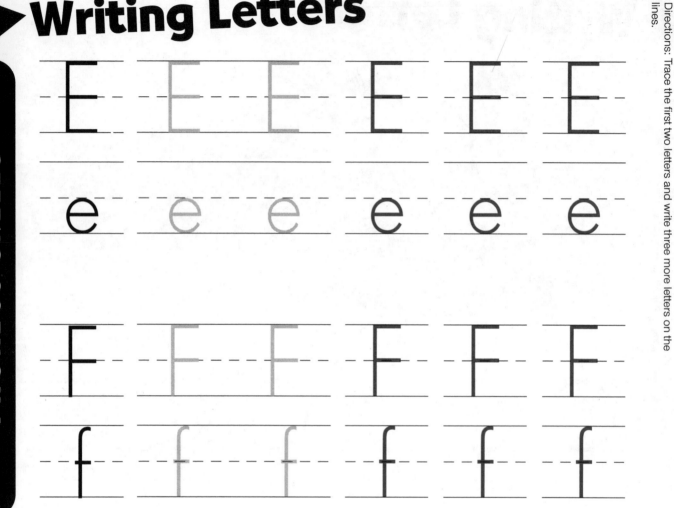

▶ **Writing Letters**

Directions: Trace the first two letters and write three more letters on the lines.

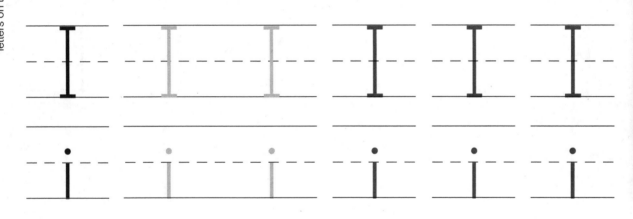

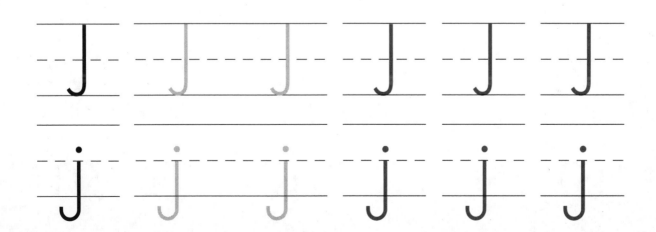

UNIT 1 Let's Read! • **Lesson 5** *Hey, Diddle, Diddle*

▶ Writing Letters

PHONICS SKILLS

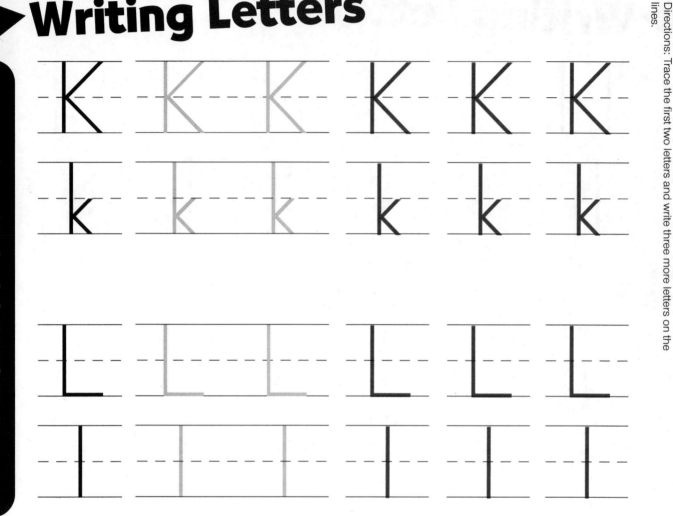

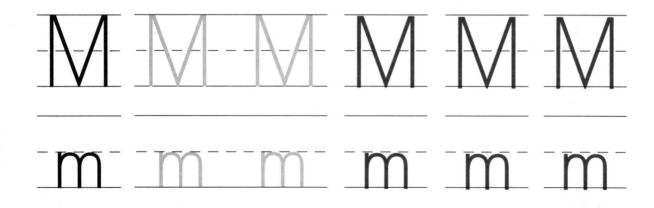

Letter Knowledge • Reteach: Phonics Skills

▶ Writing Letters

Directions: Trace the first two letters and write three more letters on the lines.

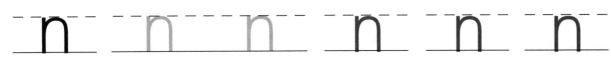

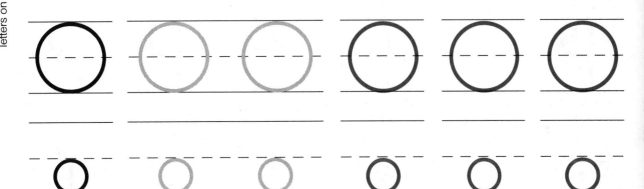

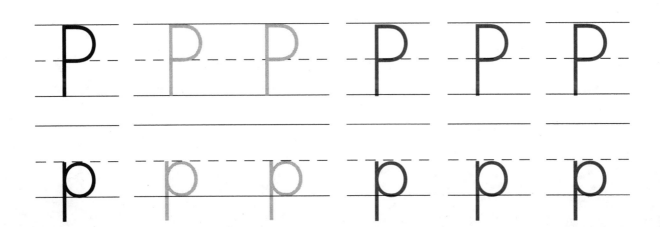

PHONICS SKILLS

▶**Writing Letters**

Directions: Trace the first two letters and write three more letters on the lines.

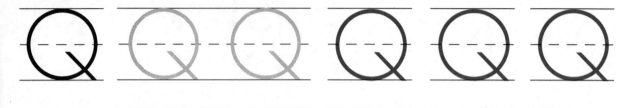

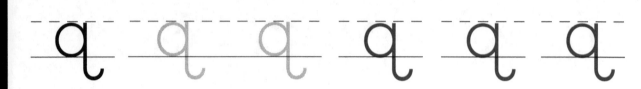

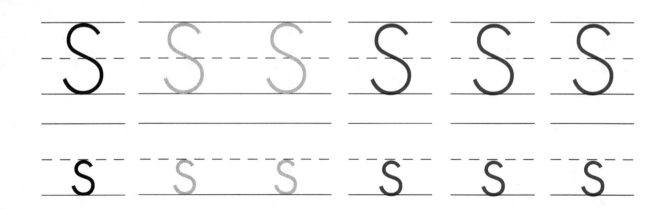

▶ Writing Letters

Directions: Trace the first two letters and write three more letters on the lines.

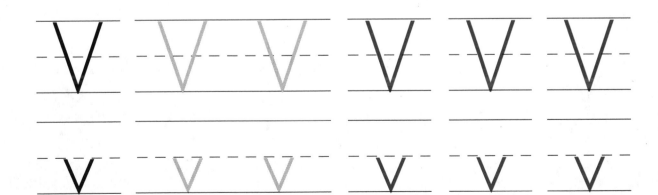

PHONICS SKILLS

UNIT 1 Let's Read! • **Lesson 9** *Rags*

▶Writing Letters

PHONICS SKILLS

Directions: Trace the first two letters and write three more letters on the lines.

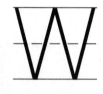  

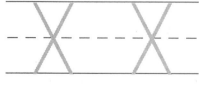  

▶ Writing Letters

PHONICS SKILLS

Directions: Trace the first two letters and write three more letters on the lines.

Y Y Y Y Y Y

y y y y y y

Z Z Z Z Z Z

Z Z Z Z Z Z

UNIT 1   Let's Read! • **Lesson 10** *Twinkle Twinkle Firefly*

▶Capital and Lowercase Letters

PHONICS SKILLS

a b c d e f g h i j k l m n o p q r s t u v w x y z
A B C D E F G H I J K L M N O P Q R S T U V W X Y Z

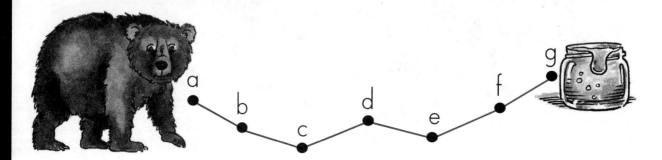

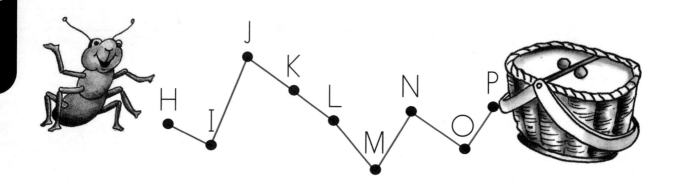

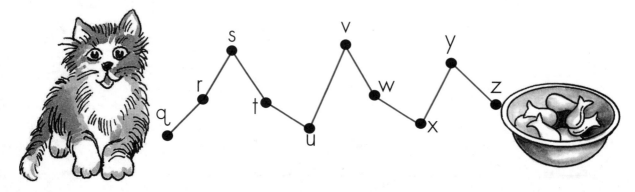

UNIT 1   Let's Read! • **Lesson 10** *Twinkle Twinkle Firefly*

▶ Capital and Lowercase Letters

a b c d e f g h i j k l m n o p q r s t u v w x y z
A B C D E F G H I J K L M N O P Q R S T U V W X Y Z

Directions: Connect the dots in order.

PHONICS SKILLS

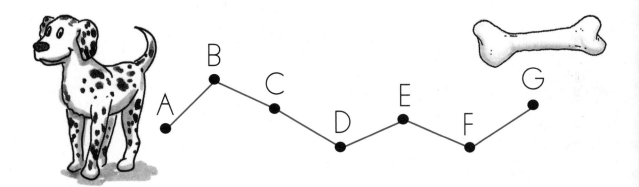

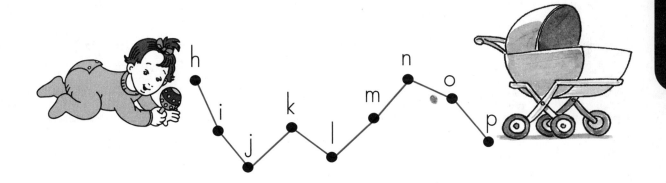

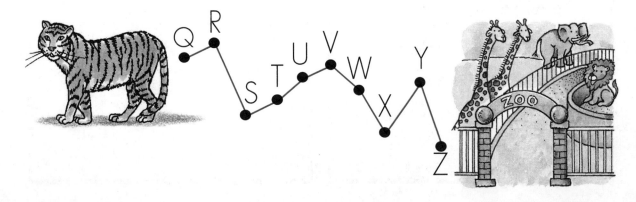

▶ **Sounds and Spellings**

Directions: Practice writing s and S. Then, draw two pictures whose names begin with the /s/ sound.

PHONICS SKILLS

S

s   s   s   s   s

S   S   S   S   S

| Answers will vary. Picture must begin with the /s/ sound. | Answers will vary. Picture must begin with the /s/ sound. |

Name _____ Date _____

▶ Sounds and Spellings

Directions: Say the name of the picture. Write a capital S next to each picture that begins with the /s/ sound.

 S

  S

 _____

 S

 S

 S

PHONICS SKILLS

▶Sounds and Spellings

Directions: Practice writing *m* and *M*. Then, draw two pictures that begin with the /m/ sound.

PHONICS SKILLS

m

    m

Answers will vary. Picture must begin with the /m/ sound.	Answers will vary. Picture must begin with the /m/ sound.

▶ Sounds and Spellings

Directions: Write a capital *M* on the line if the picture begins with the /m/ sound.

 M

 _____

 _____

 M

 M

 M

PHONICS SKILLS

►Sounds and Spellings

PHONICS SKILLS

a

Answers will vary. Picture must include the /a/ sound.	Answers will vary. Picture must include the /a/ sound.

UNIT 1   Let's Read! • **Lesson 13** *Mrs. Goose's Baby*

▶Reading and Writing

Directions: Look at the big picture. Help the students read the sentences. Have students circle the correct small picture to complete the last sentence.

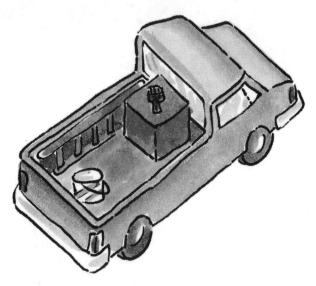

I am in the

I am on the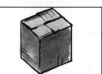

I am a _____.

I am in the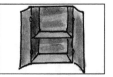

I am on the

I am a _____.

UNIT I   **Let's Read!** • **Lesson 14** *Mrs. Goose's Baby*

▶Sounds and Spellings

PHONICS SKILLS

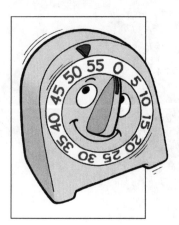

   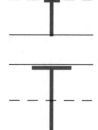

sat sat

| Answers will vary. Picture must begin with the /t/ sound. | Answers will vary. Picture must begin with the /t/ sound. |

UNIT 1 **Let's Read! • Lesson 14** *Mrs. Goose's Baby*

▶ Sounds and Spellings

Directions: Write *T* on the line if the picture begins with the /t/ sound.

PHONICS SKILLS

UNIT 1   Let's Read! • **Lesson 15** *Babybuggy*

▶Sounds and Spellings

PHONICS SKILLS

h_

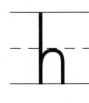

Answers will vary. Picture must begin with the /h/ sound.	Answers will vary. Picture must begin with the /h/ sound.

Directions: Practice writing *h* and *H*. Then draw two pictures whose names begin with the /h/ sound.

▶ Sounds and Spellings

Directions: Write a capital *H* on the line if the picture begins with the /h/ sound.

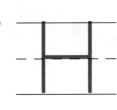
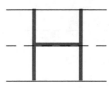

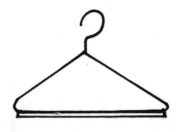
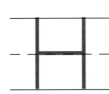

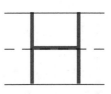

PHONICS SKILLS

UNIT 2 Animals • **Lesson 1** *Unit Introduction*

▶Sounds and Spellings

PHONICS SKILLS

p

  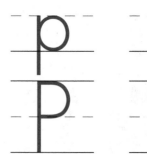

pat pat

| Answers will vary. Picture must begin with the /p/ sound. | Answers will vary. Picture must begin with the /p/ sound. |

▶Decoding

Pam has sap.
⟨Pam has a mat.⟩

⟨I tap the map.⟩
I pat the hat.

⟨Pat has a tam.⟩
Pat has a ham.

Pat has a tam.

PHONICS SKILLS

UNIT 2   Animals • **Lesson 2** *Raccoons*

▶ # Sounds and Spellings

Directions: Practice writing *i* and *I*. Copy the word. Then, draw two pictures whose names have the /i/ sound.

PHONICS SKILLS

i

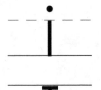

   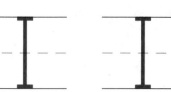

sit <u>sit</u>

| Answers will vary. Picture must have the /i/ sound. | Answers will vary. Picture must have the /i/ sound. |

▶ Writing Words

Directions: Form words by saying the sounds and writing the letters represented by each **Sound/Spelling Card** picture.

t   i   p

h   a   m

p   a   t   s

PHONICS SKILLS

▶Sounds and Spellings

Directions: Practice writing *n* and *N*. Copy the word. Then, draw two pictures whose names begin with the /n/ sound.

PHONICS SKILLS

n

n   n   n   n   n

N   N   N   N   N

nip nip

Answers will vary. Picture must begin with the /n/ sound.	Answers will vary. Picture must begin with the /n/ sound.

▶Decoding

Nan has a _____.

pan
(pin)

I am a _____.

(man)
map

It is an ___ant___.

mat
(ant)

Tim has a ___ham___.

(ham)
pan

PHONICS SKILLS

UNIT 2 Animals • **Lesson 4** *Baby Animals*

▶Sounds and Spellings

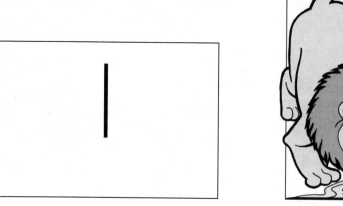

PHONICS SKILLS

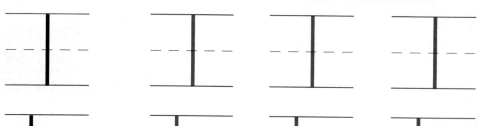

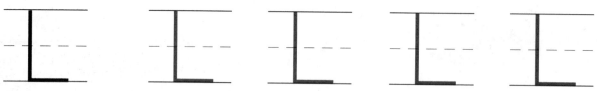

lap lap

Answers will vary. Picture must begin with the /l/ sound.	Answers will vary. Picture must begin with the /l/ sound.

30 UNIT 2 • Lesson 4   *Sounds and Spellings* • Reteach: Phonics Skills

▶Decoding

Directions: Draw a line from each word to the picture that goes with it.

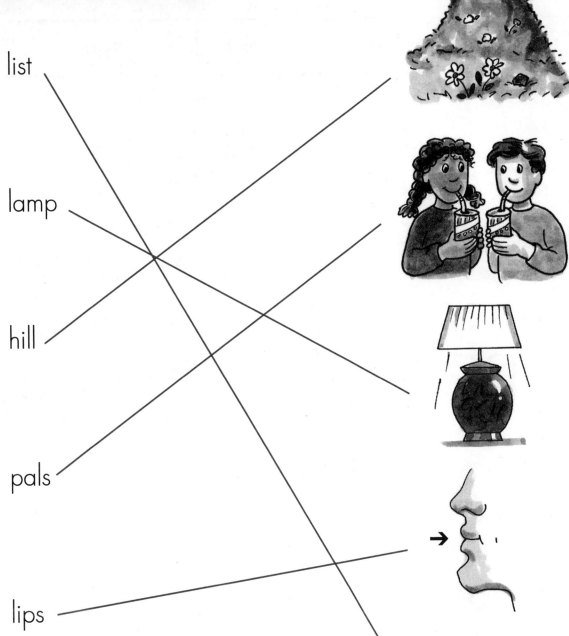

list

lamp

hill

pals

lips

▶Review

PHONICS SKILLS

hit	lamp	ant	pan

pan

ant

lamp

hit

▶Review

Directions: Look at the pictures and circle the correct word to finish each sentence. Write the correct word for the last sentence.

The ant is on a _____.

pan
(pin)

Lil has a _____.

(mitt)
map

Tim has a hat _____.

hill
(hat)

Name _____ Date _____

▶Sounds and Spellings

Directions: Practice writing *d* and *D*. Copy the word. Then, draw two pictures whose names begin with the /d/ sound.

PHONICS SKILLS

d

Answers will vary. Picture must begin with the /d/ sound.	Answers will vary. Picture must begin with the /d/ sound.

▶ Reading and Writing

Directions: Circle the word that matches the picture. Next, circle the sentence that matches the picture. Then, write the sentence.

sad

had

did

pad

Dad had a nap.

Dad hid the hat.

Dad had a nap.

PHONICS SKILLS

▶Sounds and Spellings

not

Answers will vary. Picture must have the /o/ sound.	Answers will vary. Picture must have the /o/ sound.

▶ Completing Sentences

Directions: Look at the pictures and read the sentences. Circle the correct word to complete each sentence. Write the correct word for the last one.

Mom has a _____.

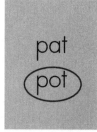

pat
(pot)

Sam did _____.

(hop)
hip

It is a mop.

map
(mop)

▶ Sounds and Spellings

PHONICS SKILLS

bat

Answers will vary. Picture must begin with the /b/ sound.	Answers will vary. Picture must begin with the /b/ sound.

▶Decoding

Directions: Circle the word or sentence that matches each picture. Then, write the sentence.

bin
(bat)

bob
(bib)

(Nan has a bat.)
Nan has a bib.

Nan has a bat.

PHONICS SKILLS

▶Sounds and Spellings

Directions: Practice writing c and C. Copy the word. Then, draw two pictures whose names begin with the /k/ sound.

PHONICS SKILLS

C

C C C C C

C C C C C

can <u>can</u>

Answers will vary. Picture must begin with the /k/ sound.	Answers will vary. Picture must begin with the /k/ sound.

UNIT 2 Animals • **Lesson 9** *Mice*

▶ Writing Words

Directions: Write the correct word under each picture. Then, circle the correct word to finish the sentence and write the word on the line.

can	cot	mat	cab

cab

can

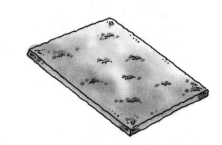

mat

cot

Dan has a cat.

cot
(cat)

▶Review

Directions: Write the word that goes with each picture.

sand	bin	dots	can

can

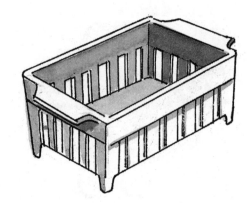

bin

sand

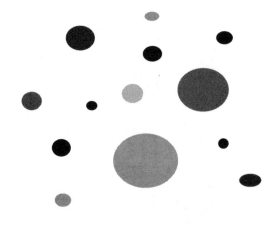

dots

Review • Reteach: Phonics Skills

Review

Nan has a _____.

can
(cap)

Tim has a _____.

(top)
tab

Pat has a <u>pin</u>.

dot
(pin)

PHONICS SKILLS

▶Sounds and Spellings

Directions: Form words by blending the consonants in the box with _ack, _ick, and _ock.

PHONICS SKILLS

c
■ ck

s	t

_ack   _ick   _ock

sack   sick   sock

tack   tick   tock

▶**Reading and Writing**

PHONICS SKILLS

Pam packs the socks.
Mick stacks the sacks.

Dick sits in the back.
Nick sits on the dock.

Nick sits on the
dock.

▶Sounds and Spellings

Directions: Practice writing *r* and *R*. Copy the word. Then, draw two pictures whose names begin with the /r/ sound.

PHONICS SKILLS

r

r   r   r   r   r

R   R   R   R   R

rat rat

| Answers will vary. Picture must begin with the /r/ sound. | Answers will vary. Picture must begin with the /r/ sound. |

▶Reading and Writing

Directions: Circle the sentence that describes the picture.
Write the sentence for the last picture.

Ron ran by the rock.
(Rick is on the ramp.)

(The rat sat on a rock.)
The ram ran by the man.

Ron rips the sack.
(A rabbit hops.)

A rabbit hops.

▶Sounds and Spellings

Directions: Practice writing *u* and *U*. Copy the word. Then, draw two pictures whose names have the /u/ sound.

PHONICS SKILLS

u

u   u   u   u   u

U   U   U   U   U

run

Answers will vary. Picture must have the /u/ sound.	Answers will vary. Picture must have the /u/ sound.

▶Reading and Writing

Directions: Circle the sentence that describes the picture.
Write the last sentence.

Bud is stuck in the mud.
(Bud picks up the pup.)

(A sub is in the tub.)
Mud is on the duck.

Pam picks up a cup.
(Pam runs for the bus.)

PHONICS SKILLS

Pam runs for the bus.

▶Sounds and Spellings

g

g g g g g

G G G G G

got <u>got</u>

| **Answers will vary. Picture must begin with the /g/ sound.** | **Answers will vary. Picture must begin with the /g/ sound.** |

Directions: Practice writing g and G. Copy the word. Then, draw two pictures whose names begin with the /g/ sound.

▶Writing Words

bag

rug

tug

gum

dog

big

gum big

PHONICS SKILLS

▶Review

Directions: Look at the pictures. Circle the correct word to finish each sentence. Write the correct word for the last one.

Bud has a _____.

big
(bag)

Nan tips the _____.

(mug)
rag

Ron has a tack.

rock
(tack)

▶Review

bun	cat	bin	cut

cut

bun

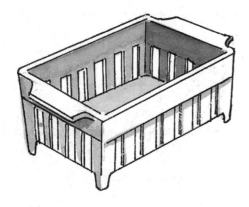

bin

cat

PHONICS SKILLS

▶ Sounds and Spellings

Directions: Practice writing *j* and *J*. Copy the words. Then, draw two pictures whose names begin with the /j/ sound.

PHONICS SKILLS

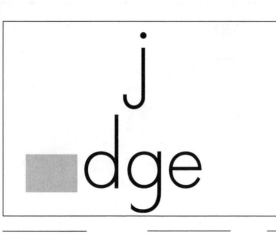

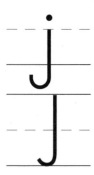 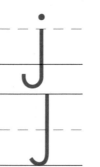 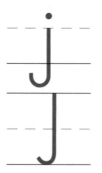 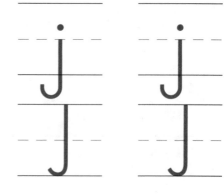

jug jug judge judge

Answers will vary. Picture must begin with the /j/ sound.	Answers will vary. Picture must begin with the /j/ sound.

▶ Decoding/Dictation

Directions: Read the two sentences, circle the sentence that describes the picture, and write the sentence on the line. Say the name of each picture to the student. Then, have the student write the name of each picture and underline the /j/ spelling.

Jim is a jam judge.
Jan can jog.

Jim is a jam judge.

jug   jump   badge

PHONICS SKILLS

▶Sounds and Spellings

Directions: Practice writing *f* and *F*. Copy the word. Then, draw two pictures whose names begin with the /f/ sound.

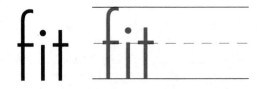

Answers will vary. Picture must begin with the /f/ sound.	**Answers will vary. Picture must begin with the /f/ sound.**

UNIT 3 **Things That Go • Lesson 2** *I Go with My Family to Grandma's*

▶Blending

Directions: Say each sound. Write the letter represented by each **Sound/Spelling Card** picture to form a word.

PHONICS SKILLS

f   i   n

f   i   s   t

c   a   m   p

▶Sounds and Spellings

PHONICS SKILLS

e

e   e   e   e   e

E   E   E   E   E

pet pet

Answers will vary. Picture must have the /e/ sound.	Answers will vary. Picture must have the /e/ sound.

▶ Sounds and Spellings

Directions: Write the correct word beside each picture. Then, write the letters for the sounds represented by the **Sound/Spelling Card** pictures. Finally, read the sentence and write the missing word.

pet	tent	bed	neck

bed

pet

tent

neck

t e n

Ted has **ten** pens.

PHONICS SKILLS

▶Review

Directions: Read the words in the box and name each picture. Then, write the correct word under each picture.

PHONICS SKILLS

| bell | fudge | left | jet |

jet

fudge

left

bell

Review • Reteach: Phonics Skills

▶Review

l	f

PHONICS SKILLS

frog

belt

log

gift

▶Sounds and Spellings

PHONICS SKILLS

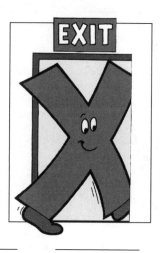

box box

Answers will vary. Picture must end with the /ks/ sound.	Answers will vary. Picture must end with the /ks/ sound.

UNIT 3 **Things That Go • Lesson 5** *I Go with My Family to Grandma's*

▶ Listening for Vowels

PHONICS SKILLS

pod   (pad)   (ox)   ax   (mitt)   mutt

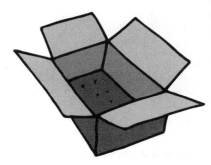

p_i_n   b_a_t   b_o_x

▶Sounds and Spellings

Directions: Practice writing z and Z. Copy the words. Then, draw a picture whose name begins with the /z/ sound.

PHONICS SKILLS

z
__s

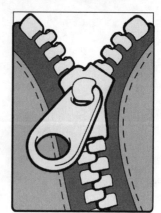

z z z z z
Z Z Z Z Z

zap zap   fuzz fuzz

Answers will vary. Picture must begin with the /z/ sound.

his his

▶ Possessives

| Jan | pig | Tim | dog |

Tim's

dog's

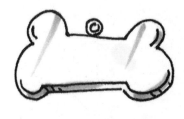

Jan's

pig's

PHONICS SKILLS

▶Review

| mix | zip | dress | six |

zip

mix

six

dress

Review • Reteach: Phonics Skills

Directions: Write the correct word under each picture.

▶Review

Max and Tess have **glass** jars.

grass
(glass)

buzz   zip   fuzz

PHONICS SKILLS

UNIT 3 **Things That Go • Lesson 8** *On the Go*

▶Sounds and Spellings

PHONICS SKILLS

sh

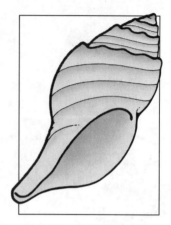

sh   sh   sh   sh   sh

Sh   Sh   Sh   Sh   Sh

ship ship

| Answers will vary. Picture must begin with the /sh/ sound. | Answers will vary. Picture must begin with the /sh/ sound. |

▶ Decoding/Blending

hush	shed	shut	fish

shut

shed

fish

hush

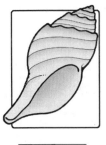   

sh   i   f   t

PHONICS SKILLS

▶ Sounds and Spellings

Directions: Practice writing *th* and *Th*. Copy the word. Then, draw two pictures whose names begin with the /th/ sound.

th

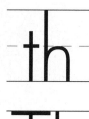

than than

| Answers will vary. Picture must begin with the /th/ sound. | Answers will vary. Picture must begin with the /th/ sound |

PHONICS SKILLS

▶Decoding/Dictation

Directions: Unscramble the words to make a sentence. Write the sentence. Say the name of each picture to the student. Have the student write the name of each picture and underline the /th/ spelling.

| shell. | Thad | a | has |

Thad has a shell.

thin   bath   path

▶Review

Directions: Practice writing *th* and *sh*. Copy the words. Then, draw two pictures: one whose name has the /th/ sound and one whose name has the /sh/ sound.

PHONICS SKILLS

th
sh

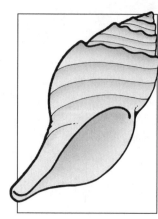

 th
 th
th
th
th

sh
sh
sh
sh
sh

then then ship ship

Answers will vary. Picture must have the /th/ sound.	**Answers will vary. Picture must have the /sh/ sound.**

Review • Reteach: Phonics Skills

▶Review

Directions: Name each picture. Write *sh* or *th* on the line to complete the word correctly.

PHONICS SKILLS

| sh | th |

thick

shop

trash

math

▶Sounds and Spellings

Directions: Practice writing *ch* and *tch*. Copy the words. Then, draw two pictures: one whose name begins with the /ch/ sound and one whose name ends with the /ch/ sound.

ch
tch

ch   ch   ch   ch   ch

tch   tch   tch   tch   tch

chip chip itch itch

Answers will vary. Picture must begin with the /ch/ sound.	Answers will vary. Picture must end with the /ch/ sound.

▶ Decoding/Dictation

Directions: Write the correct word under each picture. Say the name of each picture to the student. Have the student write the name of the picture and underline the /ch/ spelling.

| hatch | chip | pitch |

chip   pitch   hatch

chop   match   chin

PHONICS SKILLS

▶Sounds and Spellings

Directions: Practice writing ar. Copy the word. Then, draw two pictures whose names have the /ar/ sound.

PHONICS SKILLS

ar

ar   ar   ar   ar   ar

cart cart

Answers will vary. Picture must have the /ar/ sound.	Answers will vary. Picture must have the /ar/ sound.

▶Decoding

Directions: Circle the pictures whose names have the /ar/ sound. Write each word under the correct picture.

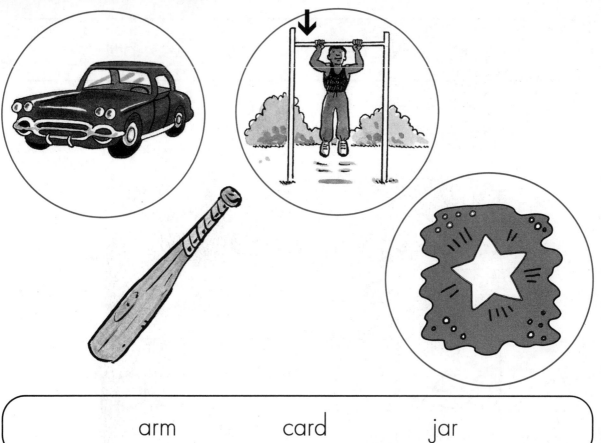

arm	card	jar

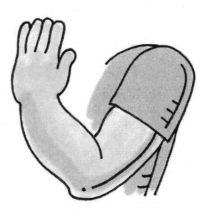

card   jar   arm

PHONICS SKILLS

▶Review

PHONICS SKILLS

| pup | bed | six | pot |

bed

pot

six

pup

▶Review

Lil can <u>catch</u>.

pitch
(catch)

sh<u>e</u>lf   ch<u>i</u>ck   ch<u>o</u>p

UNIT 3 **Things That Go** • **Lesson 14** *Trucks (Camiones)*

▶Sounds and Spellings

PHONICS SKILLS

W__

 will  will

Answers will vary. Picture must begin with the /w/ sound.	Answers will vary. Picture must begin with the /w/ sound.

UNIT 3 **Things That Go • Lesson 14** *Trucks (Camiones)*

▶ Sounds and Spellings

Directions: Practice writing *wh* and *Wh*. Copy the word. Then, draw a picture whose name begins with the /hw/ sound.

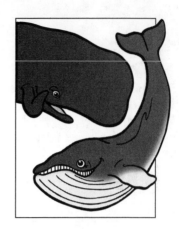

wh_

wh   wh   wh   wh

Wh   Wh   Wh   Wh

whip

Answers will vary.
Picture must begin
with the /hw/ sound.

PHONICS SKILLS

▶ Sounds and Spellings

Directions: Practice writing *er*, *ir*, and *ur*. Copy the words. Then, draw one picture whose name has the /er/ sound.

PHONICS SKILLS

er
ir
ur

er	er	er	er	er
ir	ir	ir	ir	ir
ur	ur	ur	ur	ur

herd herd

shirt shirt

Answers will vary. Picture must have the /er/ sound.

▶ Decoding/Dictation

| bird. | is | her | It |

It is her bird.

▶ Dictation

dirt   fern   hurt

PHONICS SKILLS

▶Review

PHONICS SKILLS

Directions: Write the word that goes with each picture.

| chin | her | curl | wag |

chin

curl

wag

her

▶Completing Sentences

Directions: Circle the correct word and write the name of each picture. Have the student write the name of each picture and underline the spellings of /ch/, /ar/, and /ir/.

Bob has a <u>turtle</u>.

turtle
bird

Pat sees a <u>star</u>.

star
car

▶Dictation

 patch

 car

bird

▶Sounds and Spellings

Directions: Practice writing *k* and *K*. Then, copy the words in the spaces provided. Draw two pictures whose names begin with the /k/ sound.

PHONICS SKILLS

k

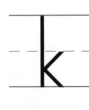

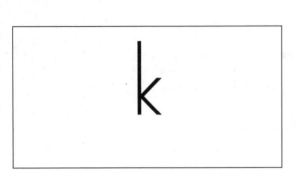 dark dark kit kit

Answers will vary. Picture must begin with the /k/ sound.	**Answers will vary. Picture must begin with the /k/ sound.**

▶ Decoding

| kitten | milk | bark | fork |

Directions: Write the word from the box that goes with each picture.

fork

bark

kitten

milk

▶Sounds and Spellings

Directions: Practice writing *ng*. Copy the words. Then draw a picture whose name ends with the /ng/ sound.

PHONICS SKILLS

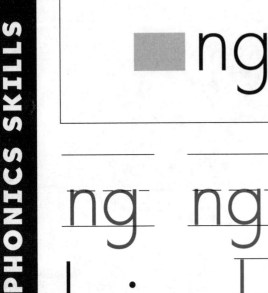

ng   ng   ng   ng

bring   bring

ring   ring

Answers will vary.

Picture must end with the /ng/ sound.

▶ Decoding/Dictation

Directions: Write the sentence shown by each picture. Say the name of each picture to the student. Have the student write the name of each picture and underline the spellings of /ng/ or /nk/.

The ring is big.
He sings.

The ring is big.

It has wings.
He swings.

He swings.

▶ **Dictation**

ring   king   sink

PHONICS SKILLS

▶ Sounds and Spellings

Directions: Practice writing *qu* and *Qu*. Then, copy the words in the spaces provided. Draw a picture that begins with the /kw/ sound.

PHONICS SKILLS

qu___

qu   qu   qu   qu

Qu   Qu   Qu   Qu

quilt   quilt   quit   quit

**Answers will vary.
Picture must begin
with the /kw/ sound.**

▶ Listening for Words

1.

quit   (quilt)

2.

squint   (squirt)

3.

A quick squirrel ran.

A quick squirrel ran.

▶Sounds and Spellings

Directions: Practice writing y and Y. Then, copy the words in the spaces provided. Draw a picture that begins with the /y/ sound.

Y—

Y Y Y Y
Y Y Y Y

yarn yarn   yell yell

Answers will vary.
Picture must begin
with the /y/ sound.

▶ Reading Sentences and Writing

Directions: Circle the sentence that matches the picture. Say the name of each picture to the student. Have the student write the name of each picture and underline the spelling of the /y/ sound.

(The cat bats the yarn.)
The man yells in the yard.

yarn

yak

yell

▶Review

| king | yarn | yak | quilt |

Directions: Write the word from the box that goes with each picture.

yak

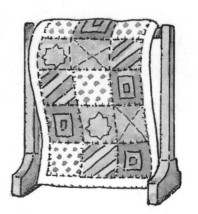

quilt

yarn

king

▶ Completing Sentences

Directions: Look at the pictures and circle the correct word to complete the sentences. Write the word for the last sentence.

She sang a  .

long
(song)

Dan has a  .

skunk
(bank)

The swing set is in the ___yard___ .

(yard)
barn

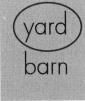

▶ Sounds and Spellings

PHONICS SKILLS

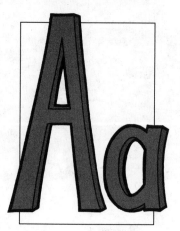

a
a__e

ate   <u>ate</u>

tape   <u>tape</u>

Words will vary but must have the /ā/ sound spelled *a* or *a_e*.

_____   _____

- - - - - - - - - - - - -   - - - - - - - - - - - - -

_____   _____

- - - - - - - - - - - - -   - - - - - - - - - - - - -

_____   _____

▶ Completing Sentences

1. Pat was  for class.

gate
(late)

2. Sam swam in the .

(lake)
flake

3. Let's play a 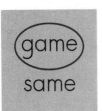 .

(game)
same

▶ Dictation

gate   rake   cake

PHONICS SKILLS

▶ Sounds and Spellings

Directions: Practice writing *ce* and *ci* and copy the words below. Then draw a picture whose name has the /s/ sound spelled *ce* or *ci_*.

PHONICS SKILLS

s
ce
ci_

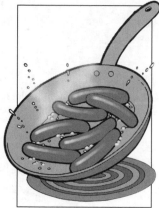

ce   ce   ce   ce

_____   _____   _____   _____

ci   ci   ci   ci

_____   _____   _____   _____

race race
_____

circle circle
_____

Answers will vary. Picture must have the /s/ sound spelled *ce* or *ci_*.

▶ Listening for Consonants

Directions: List each word under the **Sound/Spelling Card** picture for the /s/ sound or /k/ sound.

base	rake	cane	pace

base   rake

pace   cane

PHONICS SKILLS

▶Review

| tape | cane | gate | ape |

Directions: Write the word from the box that goes with each picture.

cane

gate

ape

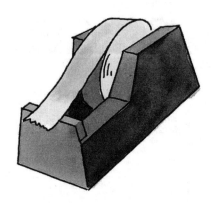

tape

▶ Writing Words

f l r

___ace face lace race

t c s

___ame tame came same

▶ Dictation

 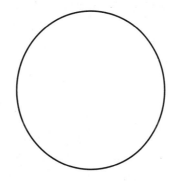 

cub circle race

▶ Sounds and Spellings

Directions: Copy the words in the spaces provided. Then write other words with the /ī/ sound spelled *i* or *i_e*.

PHONICS SKILLS

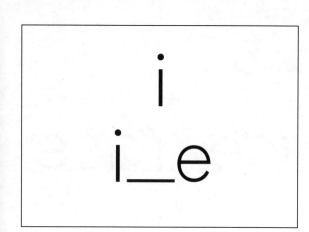

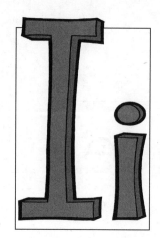

fine fine pile pile

Words will vary but must have the /ī/ sound spelled *i* or *i_e*.

_____ _____

- - - - - - - - - - - - -   - - - - - - - - - - - - -

_____ _____

- - - - - - - - - - - - -   - - - - - - - - - - - - -

_____ _____

- - - - - - - - - - - - -   - - - - - - - - - - - - -

▶Completing Sentences

PHONICS SKILLS

1. The **lime** is ripe.

limp
lime

2. We must stand in **line** .

lane
line

3. Jen rides her **bike** .

bike
bake

4. My dog does not **bite** .

bit
bite

▶ Sounds and Spellings

PHONICS SKILLS

Directions: Copy the words in the spaces provided. Then write other words with the /ō/ sound spelled o or o_e.

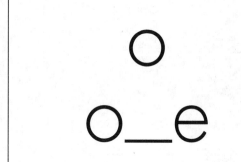

no <u>no</u>   bone <u>bone</u>

Words will vary but must have the /ō/ sound spelled *o* or *o_e*.

▶ Decoding/Dictation

rope
(hope)

I [hope] the sun is out.

(stone)
hope

Dad can lift a [stone].

▶ Dictation

cone

rope

PHONICS SKILLS

▶**Review**

PHONICS SKILLS

lime	rose	rake	plane

plane

rose

lime

rake

▶Review

Directions: Look at the pictures and circle the correct word to complete each sentence.

He made a  .

cake
rake

The girl liked to  .

file
smile

The dog ate the 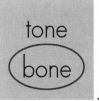 .

tone
bone

▶Review

Directions: Write the word from the box that goes with each picture. Below, say the name of each picture to the student. Have the student write the name of each picture and underline the spellings of the long-vowel sounds.

PHONICS SKILLS

| cane | bone | bike |

bike   cane   bone

▶Dictation

whale   rose   ice

▶Review

Directions: Look at the pictures and circle the correct word to finish each sentence.

The kitten wore a .

ball
(bell)

Brett has pet .

(mice)
rice

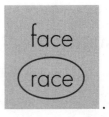

Jane ran in a .

face
(race)

PHONICS SKILLS

▶Sounds and Spellings

PHONICS SKILLS

V

V V V V V

V V V V V

vote <u>vote</u> vane <u>vane</u>

Answers will vary. Picture must begin with the /v/ sound.	**Answers will vary. Picture must begin with the /v/ sound.**

Name _____ Date _____

▶Completing Sentences

Directions: Write the correct word to finish each sentence. The first one is done for you.

PHONICS SKILLS

1. Mike drives on Vine Lane.

fives
drives

2. Viv rides in a van.

van
stove

3. I saved five nickels.

hive
five

4. Grace put the buds in the vase.

vote
vase

▶Sounds and Spellings

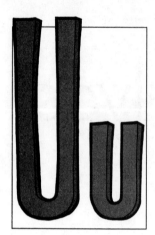

u

u__e

PHONICS SKILLS

cute cute

cube cube

**Words will vary but
must have the
/ū/ sound
spelled *u* or *u_e*.**

▶ Reading and Writing

(The ice cubes melt.)
The mule is cute.

The ice cubes melt.

▶ Dictation

music   mule   menu

▶Sounds and Spellings

j ge
gi_

ge ge ge ge ge

gi gi gi gi gi

ginger ginger

Answers will vary. Picture must have the /j/ sound spelled ge or gi_.	Answers will vary. Picture must have the /j/ sound spelled ge or gi_.

▶ Listening for Consonants

Directions: Read the words in the box. Write each word under the correct **Sound/Spelling Card.** Say the name of each picture to the student. Have the student write the name of each picture and underline the spelling of the /j/ sound.

rug	germ	game	stage

germ

rug

stage

game

gerbil   page   cage

UNIT 5 Weather • **Lesson 2** *When a Storm Comes Up*

▶ Sounds and Spellings

Directions: Copy the words. Then write other words with the /ē/ sound spelled *e* or *e_e*.

PHONICS SKILLS

e
e__e

me <u>me</u>

theme <u>theme</u>

Words will vary but must have the /ē/ sound spelled *e* or *e_e*.

▶Reading and Writing

He sang the theme song.
He broke the meter.

She will sit on a bench.
She is an athlete.

We will compete.
We sit on a trapeze.

We will compete.

PHONICS SKILLS

▶Review

Directions: Read the words in the box. Write the word that goes with each picture.

he	vase	cube	stage

stage

cube

he

vase

Review • Reteach: Phonics Skills

UNIT 5 Weather • **Lesson 3** *When a Storm Comes Up*

▶ Decoding/Dictation

Directions: Look at the pictures. Circle the correct word and then write the word in the space. Say the name of each picture to the student. Have the student write the name of each picture and underline the spellings for the /ē/ sound.

Gene has a mule .

mole (mule)

The bird is not in the cage .

(cage) page

she   we   meter

PHONICS SKILLS

UNIT 5   Weather • **Lesson 4** *When a Storm Comes Up*

Directions: Read the words in the box. Write the correct word for each picture.

PHONICS SKILLS

▶Review

| stampede   rice   cane   bugle |

cane   stampede

bugle   rice

Review • Reteach: Phonics Skills

▶ Decoding

PHONICS SKILLS

Vince turns the _____.

hedge
(page)

_____ can run fast.

(We)
He

Steve has a ___van___.

vine
(van)

▶ Sounds and Spellings

PHONICS SKILLS

ee
ea

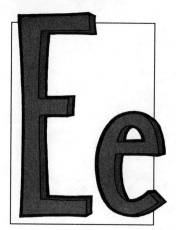

ee   ee   ee   ee   ee

ea   ea   ea   ea   ea

jeep jeep tea tea

Words will vary but must have the /ē/ sound spelled *ee* or *ea*.

UNIT 5 Weather • **Lesson 5** *When a Storm Comes Up*

▶ Writing Opposites/ Dictation

Directions: Read each word in the box. Then, write the correct word on the line next to its opposite. Say the name of each picture to the student. Have the student write the name of each picture and underline the spellings of the /ē/ sound.

| start | last | fat |

first   *last*

thin   *fat*

stop   *start*

seal   *peach*   *heel*

PHONICS SKILLS

▶Sounds and Spellings

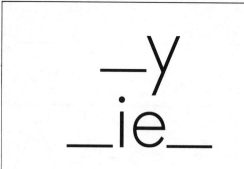

Directions: Practice writing y and *ie*. Copy the words. Then write other words with the /ē/ sound spelled _y or _ie_.

PHONICS SKILLS

y y y y y

ie ie ie ie ie

city city field field

Words will vary but must have the /ē/ sound spelled _y or _ie_.

▶ Decoding

The guppies swim in the pond.
The guppy swims in the pond.

Her niece is funny.
Her kitty is funny.

Andy eats a piece of cake.
Andy pats a bunny.

Andy pats a bunny.

PHONICS SKILLS

▶Sounds and Spellings

PHONICS SKILLS

deer	fire	hare	store

store   hare

fire   deer

▶ Decoding/Dictation

Directions: Look at the pictures. Read each sentence and the two words under the sentence. Circle the word that correctly completes the sentence. Say the name of each picture to the student. Have the student write the name of each picture and underline the long vowel spelling and *r*.

The _____ eats grass.

hare (mare)

Sam has _____ bugs.

(more) sore

__ear__

__wire__

sore

bare

▶ Sounds and Spellings

Directions: Practice writing *ai* and *ay*. Copy the words. Then write other words with the /ā/ sound spelled *ai_* or *_ay*.

PHONICS SKILLS

ai_
_ay

ai   ai   ai   ai   ai

ay   ay   ay   ay   ay

hay hay main main

Words will vary but must have the /ā/ sound spelled *ai_* or *_ay*.

▶ Decoding

hay hair

hair

fair face

fair

pair pail

pair

stare stage

stare

PHONICS SKILLS

▶ Sounds and Spellings

Directions: Practice writing *igh*. Copy the words. Then write other words with the sound /ī/ spelled *igh*.

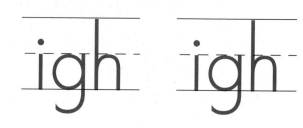

igh   igh   igh   igh

thigh   thigh   light   light

tight   tight   sigh   sigh

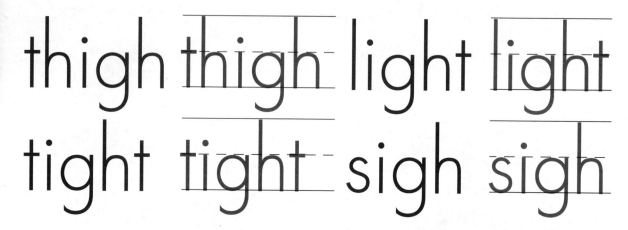

Words will vary but must have the /ī/ sound spelled *igh*.

▶ Decoding/Dictation

Directions: Draw a line to connect the two words that go together to make a compound word. Write the compound words on the lines. Say the name of each picture to the student. Have the student write the name of each picture and underline the spellings of the /ī/ sound.

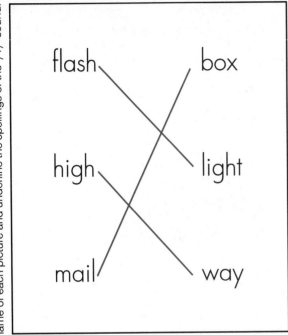

flash   box

high   light

mail   way

flashlight

highway

mailbox

night   tight   right

UNIT 5 **Weather • Lesson 10** *Clouds, Rain, Snow, and Ice*

▶Review

PHONICS SKILLS

Directions: Read the words in the box. Write the word that goes with each picture.

| city | bee | trail | tray |

tray

bee

trail

city

Review • Reteach: Phonics Skills

▶Review

Directions: Circle the correct word to finish the sentence. Write the word in the last sentence.

Lee is _____ with a hammer.

sandy
(handy)

Tammy has _____ pieces of candy.

(thirty)
zero

Katie races across the  field .

thief
(field)

Reteach: Phonics Skills • *Review*

▶ Sounds and Spellings

Directions: Practice writing y and ie. Copy the words. Then write other words with the / ī / sound spelled _y or _ie.

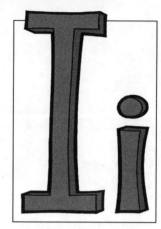

y   y   y   y   y

ie   ie   ie   ie   ie

fry fry   tie tie

Words will vary but must have the /ī/ sound spelled _y or _ie.

Name _____ Date _____

▶ Decoding/Dictation

| lie | pie | dries |

1. I like apple **pie**.

2. Jill **dries** her hair.

3. Ty never tells a **lie**.

fry   **cry**   **spy**

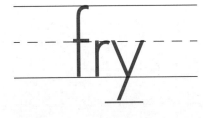

PHONICS SKILLS

▶ Sounds and Spellings

Directions: Practice writing o and oe. Copy the words. Then write four other words with the /ō/ sound spelled o or _oe.

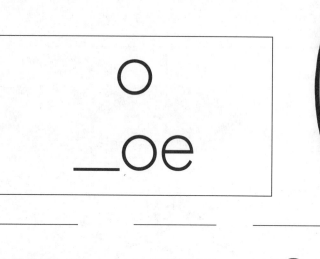
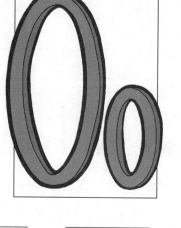

o
_oe

o   o   o   o   o

oe   oe   oe   oe   oe

go go   hoe hoe

Words will vary but must have the /ō/ sound
spelled *o* or *_oe*.

_____

_____

Sounds and Spellings • Reteach: Phonics Skills

▶Decoding

Directions: Read the words in each box. Fill in the circle next to each word that has the /ō/ sound. Complete the sentence using the letters represented in the *Sound/Spelling Cards.*

● home
● cove
○ dot

● stove
○ lock
● hoe

● go
● so
● rose

g

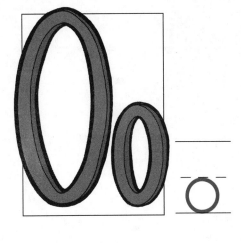

o

Joe will go to get the hoe.

▶ Sounds and Spellings

PHONICS SKILLS

Directions: Practice writing oa. Copy the word. Say the name of each picture to the student. Have the student write the name of each picture and underline the spelling of the /ō/ sound.

o
oa_

oa   oa   oa   oa   oa

boat boat

road   goat   float

Sounds and Spellings • Reteach: Phonics Skills

▶ Sounds and Spellings

```
 o
_ow
```

OW   OW   OW   OW   OW

mow mow

grow grow

Words will vary but must have the /ō/ sound spelled *oa_* or *_ow*.

PHONICS SKILLS

▶Sounds and Spellings

Directions: Practice writing ew and ue. Copy the words. Then write other words with the /ū/ sound spelled u, _ew, or _ue.

PHONICS SKILLS

u __ew
__ue

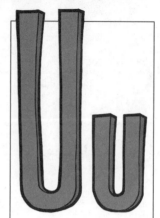

ew   ew   ew   ew   ew

ue   ue   ue   ue   ue

pew pew cue cue

Words will vary but must have the /ū/ sound
spelled *u, _ew,* or *_ue.*

▶Decoding

Directions: Read the words in the box. Look at the pictures and read the sentences. Fill in the blank with the correct word.

value	rescue	few

1. A __few__ leaves fell by the birdbath.

2. Sally will __value__ the card you made.

3. Who will __rescue__ the cat in the tree?

PHONICS SKILLS

Reteach: Phonics Skills • *Decoding*   UNIT 5 • Lesson 14   **141**

▶Review

Directions: Read the words in the box. Write the correct word on each line.

PHONICS SKILLS

| pie | hoe | goat | pry |

_____

goat

_____

pry

_____

hoe

_____

pie

UNIT 5 Weather • **Lesson 15** *Unit Wrap-Up*

▶ Decoding/Dictation

low
(glow)

The campfire will _____.

mo̲w

ro̲w

bo̲w

PHONICS SKILLS

Directions: Copy the words in the spaces provided. Then, draw two pictures whose names have the /o͞o/ sound.

▶ Sounds and Spellings

PHONICS SKILLS

oo   u_e

_ue   _ew

u

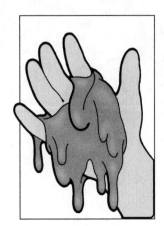

soon soon   rude rude

clue clue   blew blew

Answers will vary. Picture must have the /o͞o/ sound.	Answers will vary. Picture must have the /o͞o/ sound.

▶ Decoding/Dictation

1. Dad has a (new) set of (tools).

2. In (June)(Sue) went to the (zoo).

3. (Luke) plays the (tuba) at (noon).

PHONICS SKILLS

moon   stool   tooth

Name _____ Date _____

UNIT 6 Journeys • **Lesson 2** *Captain Bill Pinkney's Journey*

▶ Sounds and Spellings

PHONICS SKILLS

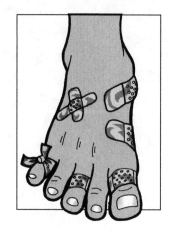

oo

oo   oo   oo   oo   oo

look look

wood wood

Answers will vary. Picture must have the /oo/ sound.	Answers will vary. Picture must have the /oo/ sound.

▶ Decoding

Directions: Circle the sentence that tells about the picture. Write the last sentence that is correct.

Luke has a good book.
Luke stood in line.

Fish splash in a brook.
Fred soaks his foot.

Sam fixes the hook.
Sam stacks wood.

PHONICS SKILLS

Sam stacks wood.

▶Review

Directions: Read the words in the box. Write the correct word under each picture.

PHONICS SKILLS

| spool | prune | chew | broom |

prune

spool

broom

chew

▶ Review

Sue has a _____ vase.

Bob has a _____ shirt.

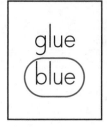

glue
(blue)

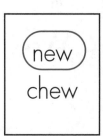

(new)
chew

PHONICS SKILLS

pl_u_me

st_e_w

b_oo_t

▶Sounds and Spellings

Directions: Practice writing ow. Copy the words. Then draw two pictures whose names have the /ow/ sound.

PHONICS SKILLS

ow

ow   ow   ow   ow   ow

down   down

crown   crown

Answers will vary. Picture must have the /ow/ sound.	Answers will vary. Picture must have the /ow/ sound.

▶ Decoding

now   pow   (plow)

town   (down)   gown

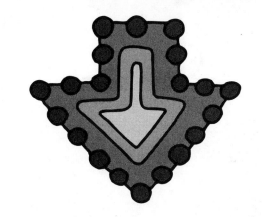

growl   crowd   (howl)

(clown)   brown   crown

howl

clown

PHONICS SKILLS

▶ Sounds and Spellings

PHONICS SKILLS

ou__

ou   ou   ou   ou   ou

trout   trout

mouth   mouth

| Answers will vary. Picture must have the /ow/ sound. | Answers will vary. Picture must have the /ow/ sound. |

▶Decoding

row	brown	tow	down

1. This truck will **tow** our car.

2. Let's slide **down** this hill.

3. Jill can **row** the boat across the lake.

4. A **brown** pup chases the ball.

down         **tow**

brown   **row**

PHONICS SKILLS

▶**Review**

PHONICS SKILLS

| cloud | growl | pound | frown |

pound

cloud

frown

growl

Review • Reteach: Phonics Skills

Name _____   Date _____

UNIT 6   **Journeys • Lesson 6** *Me on the Map*

▶Review

Directions: Circle the *ou* and *ow* words in the story. Then write each word in the correct column beside the correct sound/spelling.

Rusty is Grandpa's old (hound). One day Grandpa and Rusty walked (down) to the pond. Rusty had his bone in his (mouth). He dropped the bone. He (howled) and started to dig in the (ground). Rusty dug until there was a (mound) of dirt beside the hole. He put his bone in the hole. Then they finished the walk.

PHONICS SKILLS

hound   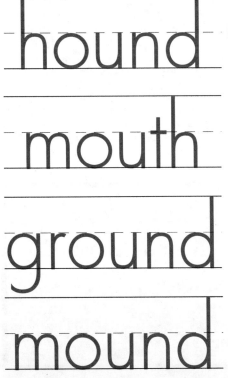   down

ou_   ow

mouth   howled

ground

mound

Reteach: Phonics Skills • *Review*   UNIT 6 • Lesson 6   **155**

▶ Sounds and Spellings

Directions: Practice writing aw and au. Copy the words. Then draw two pictures whose names have the /aw/ sound.

aw
au_

aw aw aw aw aw

au au au au au

law law sauce sauce

Answers will vary. Picture must have the /aw/ sound.	Answers will vary. Picture must have the /aw/ sound.

▶Decoding/Dictation

Directions: Circle the correct word to complete each sentence. Below, say the name of each picture for the student. Have them write the name of each picture and underline the spelling of the /aw/ sound.

Dad put the salt in the ____.

(sauce)
fault

The **hawk** swooped down.

flaw
(hawk)

saw   fawn   haul

Reteach: Phonics Skills • *Decoding/Dictation*   UNIT 6 • Lesson 7   **157**

PHONICS SKILLS

▶Review

Directions: Look at each picture and read the two sentences. Circle the sentence that goes with the picture and write the last correct sentence.

Ellie has a gown for her mom.

(Ellie has a crown for her mom.)

(Eddie sat in the straw.)

Eddie sees the fawn.

Candy draws a hawk.

(Candy uses a saw.)

Candy uses a saw.

▶**Review**

PHONICS SKILLS

mound

hound, ground

pound   (dawn)   sound

(crow)   paw   raw

growl   owl   (yawn)

UNIT 6   Journeys • **Lesson 9** *Me on the Map*

▶ Sounds and Spellings

Directions: Practice writing *kn*. Copy the words. Then say the name of each picture to the students. Have them write the name of each picture and underline the spelling of the /n/ sound.

PHONICS SKILLS

$kn\_\overset{n}{}$

kn   kn   kn   kn   kn

knee knee knot knot

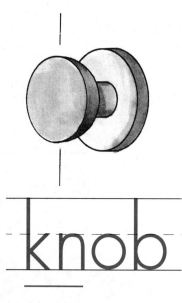

knob   knit   knife

▶ Decoding

knob	knife	knew

1. Mom cuts the pie with a __knife__.

2. Jill __knew__ how to plant flowers.

3. Just turn the __knob__.

PHONICS SKILLS

▶**Review**

Directions: Read the words in the box. Write the correct word under each picture.

| pool | brook | zoo | foot |

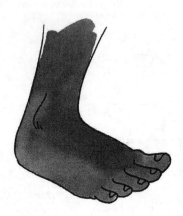

foot

pool

zoo

brook

Review • Reteach: Phonics Skills

▶Review

PHONICS SKILLS

_____ at that bright star!

Loom
(Look)

Meg can sit on this _____.

(stool)
stood

Did you hear an owl hoot ?

hood
(hoot)

PHONICS SKILLS

Directions: Number each set of words in order from 1–3. The first one is done for you.

▶Comparative Endings: –er, –est

2 longer

3 longest

1 long

2 smaller

1 small

3 smallest

1 fast

3 fastest

2 faster

▶ Decoding/Dictation

Directions: Circle the word that correctly completes each sentence. Below, say the name of each picture for the students. Have them write the name of each picture that has an arrow.

The puppy is the _____ of all.

soft   softer   (softest)

The blanket is _____ than the sheet.

thick   (thicker)   thickest

→

fuller

←

dirtiest

PHONICS SKILLS

▶Sounds and Spellings

Directions: Practice writing *oi* and *oy*. Copy the words. Then draw two pictures whose names have the /oi/ sound.

oi
_oy

oi oi oi oi oi

oy oy oy oy oy

boy boy   join join

Answers will vary. **Picture must have the** **/oi/ sound.**	**Answers will vary.** **Picture must have the** **/oi/ sound.**

▶ Decoding

spoil	hoist	join

1. Mike wants to **join** the team.

2. Bill can **hoist** the boxes into the truck.

3. The rain did not **spoil** the picnic.

PHONICS SKILLS

▶ Sounds and Spellings

Directions: Practice writing wr. Copy the words. Say the name of each picture for the students. Have them write the name of each picture and underline the spelling of the /r/ sound.

PHONICS SKILLS

r
wr__

wr   wr   wr   wr   wr

_____

wren wren write write

wring wrench wrote

Sounds and Spellings • Reteach: Phonics Skills

▶Decoding

Directions: Read the words in the box. Write the correct word from the box under each picture.

| wrong | wren | wrestler | wrecker |

_____
wren

_____
wrecker

_____
wrong

_____
wrestler

Directions: Practice writing *ph*. Copy the words. Then draw two pictures whose names have the /f/ sound.

► **Sounds and Spellings**

PHONICS SKILLS

f
ph

ph   ph   ph   ph   ph

phrase phrase

trophy trophy

Answers will vary. Picture must have the /f/ sound.

Answers will vary. Picture must have the /f/ sound.

▶ Decoding

| phone | typhoon | pheasant | photo |

Directions: Write the correct word from the box under each picture.

photo

phone

typhoon

pheasant

PHONICS SKILLS

▶**Review**

Directions: Read the words in the box. Write the correct word to complete each sentence.

PHONICS SKILLS

wren	coil	choice	gopher

1. A gopher digs a tunnel under the fence.

2. A worm can coil into a ball.

3. Bob has a choice of pie or cake.

4. A tiny wren chirps in its nest.

Review • Reteach: Phonics Skills

▶ Decoding/Dictation

Directions: Circle the word that does not belong. Below, say the name of each picture for the students. Have them write the name of each picture and underline the spelling of the /r/ sound.

1. (race) wren   wrench

2. photo   phrase (fast)

3. hoist (joy) moist

PHONICS SKILLS

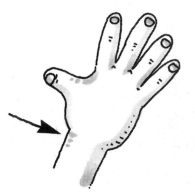

wrench wrist wreath

▶Short Vowel Sounds

▶**Circle the words with short vowel sounds. Write them under the picture with the same sound.**

PHONICS SKILLS

1. A (bug) (is) (on) the leaf.

2. (Ted) saw a (fish).

3. Kate ate the (red) (apple).

4. The (cat) (runs) by the (rock).

apple

Ted

is

cat

red

fish

on

bug

rock

runs

UNIT 7   Keep Trying • **Lesson 2** *The Itsy Bitsy Spider*

▶Long Vowel Sounds

▶Circle the words with long vowel sounds. Write them under the correct picture.

1. Dad (made) a (cute) box.
2. Tess will (need) a (pail.)
3. The dog (likes) to (eat) (bones.)
4. Tad will (use) a (light) and a (rope.)

Aa

made

pail

Ee

need

eat

Ii

likes

light

Oo

bones

rope

Uu

cute

use

▶*o* Other than Short/Long *o*

▶Write the correct word in each space.

| one | above | coming | dove | another |

1. She is the ___one___ with the green hat.

2. Look ___above___ the door for the number.

3. The white ___dove___ flew away.

4. Dale is ___coming___ home today.

5. Do you have ___another___ book?

▶ *o* Other than Short/Long *o*

▶ **Circle the correct word. Write it in the space.**

1. I like __some__ of the animals at the zoo.

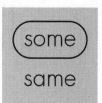

2. Do you __wonder__ why the sky is blue?

3. The trip is on __Monday__.

4. Tad __won__ the golf game.

5. When will you be __done__?

PHONICS SKILLS

PHONICS SKILLS

▶ -alk and -all

▶ **Write *alk*. Match each word with the correct picture.**

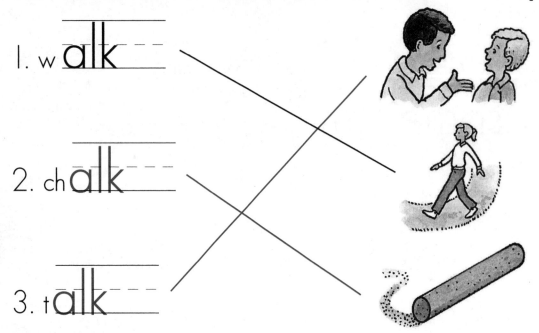

1. w alk

2. ch alk

3. t alk

▶ **Write *all*. Match each word with the correct picture.**

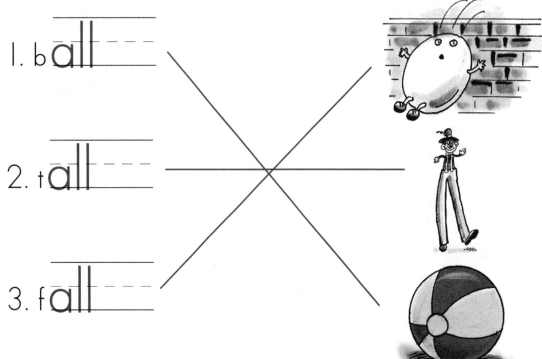

1. b all

2. t all

3. f all

▶ *-alk and -all*

▶ **Circle the correct word. Write it in the space.**

1. Jane had a __small__ cut on her hand.

   (small) stall

2. We got ice cream at the __mall__.

   malt (mall)

3. The __stalk__ broke when the plant fell.

   (stalk) stall

4. Can we take the dog for a __walk__?

   wall (walk)

5. Rob shut the gate to the horse's __stall__.

   (stall) small

PHONICS SKILLS

▶ o̅o̅ and u̅

▶ Write *oo* or *u* to complete each word.

m_u_sic

b_oo_m

st_oo_l

men_u_

r_oo_ts

b_u_gle

PHONICS SKILLS

▶ō̄o and ū

▶ **Circle the word that is spelled correctly. Write it in the space.**

1. Please fill the ice **cube** tray.

    (cube) coob

2. A lot of **food** was on the table.

    fude (food)

3. We like to ride our **mule**.

    mool (mule)

4. Do you know where your **room** is?

    (room) rume

5. Harry dropped his **spoon** in his milk.

    spune (spoon)

PHONICS SKILLS

▶/aw/ Spelled *augh*, *au_*

▶**Write *au*. Then write the word in the space.**

1. bec au se   because

2. s au ce   sauce

3. v au lt   vault

▶**Write *augh*. Then write the word in the space.**

1. c augh t   caught

2. d augh ter   daughter

3. t augh t   taught

UNIT 8 Games • **Lesson I** *Unit Introduction*

▶ /aw/ Spelled *augh, au_*

▶ **Circle the word spelled correctly.**
Write it in the space.

1. The dog __caught__ the ball.

   cot (caught)

2. The cat drank from the __saucer__ of milk.

   (saucer) soser

3. Dad did the __laundry__ today.

   londry (laundry)

4. The play got loud __applause__.

   aplose (applause)

5. She __taught__ the class how to make yogurt.

   (taught) tat

▶ /j/ and /g/

▶ **Read the paragraph. Write the underlined words under the correct picture.**

Grace's Zoo

Grace's bedroom looks like a zoo.
She has a giant gerbil in a cage. On her
desk is a tank of ten goldfish. She also
got a gentle bird as a gift from her mom.
Grace likes to be a zookeeper.

giant   cage

gerbil   gentle

PHONICS SKILLS

▶ /j/ and /g/

Grace's

goldfish

got

gift

▶ Special Spelling Patterns wa, mb

▶ **Write the correct word in each space.**

1. Is the __lamb__ with its mother?

   lamb   yam

2. Did you __wash__ your hands?

   wish   wash

3. The bird ate the __crumb__ of food.

   crunch   crumb

4. I want to have a glass of __water__.

   water   waiter

▶Special Spelling Patterns *wa, mb*

▶Circle the sentence that goes with each picture.
Write the last sentence on the line.

Mom gave Ben a new wallet.

(Mom gave Ben a new watch.)

The cat has a limp.

(The cat is on the limb.)

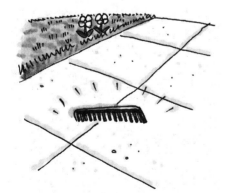

(The comb is on the sidewalk.)

The cone is on the sidewalk.

The comb is on the sidewalk.

PHONICS SKILLS

▶ /ī/ Spellings

▶ **Circle the words with the long *i* sound. Write each word one time in the spaces.**

One (night,) Heather and Kate stayed

in a (white) tent. They had a (campfire). It

made a (bright) glow. Soon the girls went to

sleep.

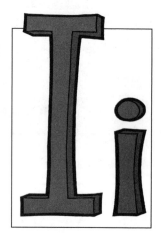

night   campfire

white   bright

▶ /e/ **Spelled _ea_**

▶**Write the words that rhyme.**

| weather   dread   leather   steady   ahead |

feather — weather — leather

bread — dread — ahead

ready — steady

PHONICS SKILLS

▶/ū/ **Spellings**

▶ **Circle the words with the long *u* sound. Write each word one time in the spaces.**

Bobby plays (music) on his (bugle). He can play a (few) happy songs to (amuse) his mom and dad. Bobby wants to be in a (huge) band and wear a (uniform) when he gets older.

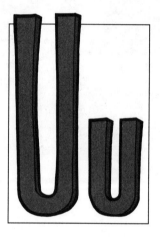

music   huge

bugle   amuse

few   uniform

▶ /ū/ Spellings

▶ **Circle the word that completes each sentence.**

1. Do they have the (**cure** cute) for a cold?

2. How much (**fuel** fuse) is left in the boat?

3. I can make a (cute **cube**) out of paper.

4. Jackie likes all kinds of (**music** muddy).

5. The (**mule** mile) walked up the path.

▶ /oo/ and /o͞o/

▶ **Circle the words with the same vowel sounds as foot or goo. List each word one time below the correct picture.**

Steve's Loose Tooth

Steve lost his (loose) (tooth) when he stubbed his (foot) and fell at the (zoo). He (took) the (tooth) home. His mom (looked) at the (tooth). Steve put the (tooth) in a little (wooden) box in his (room). (Soon) Steve will show his (tooth) to his dad.

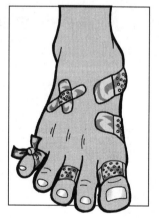

foot   looked

took   wooden

▶ /oo/ and /o͞o/

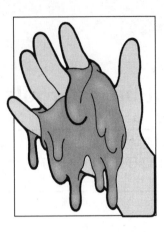

loose

tooth

zoo

room

soon

PHONICS SKILLS

▶ Long Vowels Followed by *r*

▶ **Write the word that best completes each sentence.**

share	deer	more	fair

1. The baby cried for __more__ milk.

2. Will you __share__ your books with your brother?

3. The __deer__ ran out from the woods.

4. The children had fun at the __fair__.

▶Long Vowels Followed by *r*

▶Circle the sentence that matches each picture.
Write the last sentence on the line.

PHONICS SKILLS

Chase has a sore leg.
Chase has a store leg.

Misty goes to the store.
Misty goes to the shore.

Ed drew a pickle of his dog.
Ed drew a picture of his dog.

Ed drew a picture of his dog.

PHONICS SKILLS

►Vowel Spellings in Syllables

►Write the word that best completes each sentence. The first one has been done for you.

> dinner   rattle   bugle   Summer   handle

1. The baby grabbed the __rattle__.

2. The man blew the __bugle__ each morning.

3. We had ham sandwiches for __dinner__.

4. The __handle__ came off the broom.

5. __Summer__ is the best time of the year.

▶Soft g and c

▶Write the words that rhyme. The first one has been done for you.

nice	hedge	glance	range
strange	prance	slice	ledge

dance   glance   prance

ice   nice   slice

change   strange   range

edge   hedge   ledge

PHONICS SKILLS

▶ /ē/ Spelled _ey

▶ **Write *ey*. Then write the word in the space.
Match it with the correct picture. The
first one has been done for you.**

1. hon

2. vall

3. mon

4. donk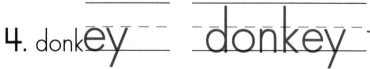

5. jock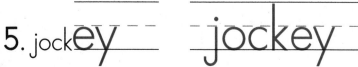

▶ /ē/ Spelled _ey

▶ **Circle the word spelled correctly. Write the word in the space.**

1. The ___monkey___ jumped into the tree.

monky (monkey)

2. The ___hockey___ player got hurt.

(hockey) hocky

3. The ___turkey___ pecked at some grain.

turky (turkey)

4. Do not forget your ___key___.

kee (key)

5. A ___kidney___ is part of your body.

(kidney) kidny

PHONICS SKILLS

▶Special Spelling Patterns: –tion, –ion

PHONICS SKILLS

▶Write *–ion* or *–tion* in each space to complete the word. The first one has been done for you.

1. My dog is a good compan‗ion‗ for me.

2. That kind of shirt is in fash‗ion‗.

3. Mason won the race and was the champ‗ion‗.

4. You are getting an educa‗tion‗.

5. Don't men‗tion‗ the price of the gift.

▶Special Spelling Patterns: –tion, –ion

▶Write the words that rhyme. The first one has been done for you.

million	location	stallion	motion	rejection

1. protection <u>rejection</u>

2. scallion <u>stallion</u>

3. trillion <u>million</u>

4. sensation <u>location</u>

5. potion <u>motion</u>